I0698278

Hey, there's a deer in my yard!

A short Saskatchewan story.

Photos & Written by

Susan Hathiramani

ISBN: 9798411204537
Imprint: Independently published

All things bright and beautiful

All creatures great and small

All things wise and wonderful,

The Lord God made them all.

~Cecil Frances Alexander

Contents

Hey, there's a deer in my yard!

The "Wee One"

It was January 4, 2022. A bitterly cold day on the prairies.

Susan finished putting away the Christmas tree; there were just the ornaments that needed to be carefully packed away. She thought to herself, I wish the magical feelings that Christmastime brings would stay with me throughout the chilly months of January and February. She picked up the delicate snowglobe in her hands.

Susan gazed at the little boy, James, with his Snowman preparing for take-off.

She shook the snow globe with care.

At the age of sixty, she felt enchanted while watching the snow gently float like soft white feathers to the bottom of the globe.

Susan poured a cup of coffee and sat in her enormous comfy pink chair with her cat, Snipper.

She decided to read the storybook, "The Snowman", and play the CD for herself and the pets.

Susan loved the loved Christmas story. Her favourite part was when James flew through the air with his Snowman.

"And they were joined by other snowmen, and they flew to the North Pole to meet Father Christmas."

Susan smiled to herself as she read the story to Leif and Snipper.

"Just in time," smiled Father Christmas.

"The party is about to start."

And what a party it was!

"James and the Snowman danced all night long!"

Suddenly, Susan's dog, Leif, started to bark.

She went to the window, and the fawn gazed back at her.

The little one's sweet face was covered with frost. And it seemed to be starving.

She went to the fridge, "I wonder what I can feed the "Wee one"?"

Susan put on her warmest coat, scarf, and winter boots. She walked around the deck and placed the food where the little one could find the fruit and vegetables.

The fawn darted! And it ran back into the grove of pine trees in her backyard.

"Oh, dear," "I have scared it off!"

Susan peered through the patio doors. Then she settled back into her chair and read the story to her fur babies.

Snipper jumped back into her lap and began to purr.

"I love this part of the story too," she said to Snipper.

"As the first rays of sunlight appeared over the hills. Father Christmas handed James a parcel."

"For me?" James gasped.

"It was a soft blue scarf, beautifully decorated with snowmen."

"Oh, thank you!" cried James.

"He gave Father Christmas a big hug. And then it was time to go."

Leif began barking again. "What is it, doggo?" Susan asked her dog.

Leif went over to the patio doors. He sat down and barked once more at the fawn as it looked back through the window at him.

Susan shouted, "the little one is back. She grabbed her phone and snapped photos of the fawn.

After the deer had finished its feast, he walked off the deck and wandered back to the pine grove.

Susan decided to share the photos on Facebook after the excitement was over.

Then she went back to reading the storybook.

Leif laid down by her feet. And the cat snuggled back into her lap.

"This is the best part of the story, Leif and Snipper!" Susan read the last part of the story to her pets.

"James and the Snowman soared into the air and flew towards home."

"When they arrived, it was nearly morning and time for James to go back to bed."

"James did not want to leave his friend, but he knew it was time to say goodbye."

"With one last look at the Snowman, James went inside and upstairs to bed."

"Happy and exhausted, he fell asleep."

Leif jumped up, and Susan saw that the fawn was looking through their living room.

"Well," "Wee one", I would like to finish reading my story."

"So, finish your lunch and enjoy listening to the tale."

"In the morning, James's first thought was of the Snowman."

"He jumped out of bed and raced down the stairs, past Mum and Dad…out of the door, and into the garden."

"But the Snowman had gone."

"Well, Leif and Snipper, that is the end of my favourite Christmas story!"

Susan rose out of her chair and saw that the deer was gone. She closed the drapes and wondered if the little one would come back?

Sure enough, the next day, the fawn was back in her yard and looking for more food. She decided to name the fawn "Sunflower" since the deer had soft brown eyes with petal-like markings above its eyes.

Susan fed the fawn each day; Apples, sunflower seeds, and carrots.

When the weather warmed up, Susan went out to the yard with Leif and built a snowman. She created a snowman that looked like Jame's Snowman in the storybook.

"There you go, 'Wee ones', now you have a snowman to protect you when I am at work!"

Also, many more deer came to visit over the winter months. Susan fed the deer and birds that came to visit.

The magic feelings of Christmastime stayed with Susan until the first signs of springtime arrived.

The "Wee one" was gone, and the rest of the deer too. When Susan was driving home to the village of Annaheim, she saw several deer leaving the village. The deer looked happy and free because they were running out to the fields where the green grass was starting to poke through the last bit of the snow.

When Susan arrived at her house, She stood outside and listened to the Chickadees singing, "Sweet Spring". She saw that her Snowman had melted.

The green scarf, hat, and black buttons lay on the ground.

Susan picked up the tangerine nose that belonged to the Snowman and put it into the compost bin. She softly whispered to her Snowman—Goodbye, old friend.

She smiled at the cherished memories of the fawns that became part of her family during the winter months.

Susan opened the front door, and Leif greeted her with licks and a wagging tail. She made a pot of coffee and waited for it to brew.

She poured a cup of coffee and played the piece of music, "***Walking in the air***" by Howard Blake.

Susan felt relaxed and finally fell asleep in her armchair while dreaming of the Snowman flying through the air with James. And the fawns that were eating green grass in the nearby fields.

Snipper snuggled into her lap. And Leif curled up beside her feet.

"James and his snowman start running as fast as they can. And soon they are flying through the air to the North Pole!"

The first morning the fawn appeared in my front yard

The first day the fawn came for a visit!

**They are finding shelter beneath the "Gabby"
Tree.**

Do you have some carrots or apples?

They are enjoying eating the sunflower seeds.

Today, I'm feeling a bit camera shy!

"Hey lady, what's for breakfast?"

Hey, there's a deer in my yard!

I just stopped by for some lunch.

**Hey Mom, there is a deer is looking through the
window!**

Hey, there's a deer in my yard!

I need some food too?

The beginning of the blizzard. February 1, 2022.

The snowman watches over the 'wee ones' during the blizzard.

Hey, there's a deer in my yard!

Waiting for more apples.

The "Wee one" eating apples.

A mama deer with her twin fawns.

The twins are enjoying a feast of sunflower seeds.

Good Night, sweet baby! March 1, 2022.

Hey, there's a deer in my yard!

Eating Buns!

Snipper meets a deer friend!

Hey, there's a deer in my yard!

We just dropped by for some breakfast!

I would like some more food please!

Easter morning. Goodbye my friends. April 17, 2022

Author: Susan Hathiramani

"Many white-tailed deer stayed in our village during January, February and March.

I saw the deer leaving the village just after the Easter holiday.

"The best I could do for the deer is feed them sunflower seeds, apples, carrots and leftover vegetables."

"The hardest part was watching over the fawns, who did not have a mom to care for them."

Sadly, one morning in late February, we had to call the Conservation officer to come from LeRoy, Saskatchewan, to assist with one of the fawns that had been injured.

My friend Trina and I cried when we found out the little fawn would have to be put down. It took a couple of days to recover from the loss.

Yet, each day, more fawns wandered into the yard. Yes, these wee ones are wild animals, and it is hard to protect them from their natural predators.

It is the first time; I have experienced such an abundance of hungry deer staying in my village.

Thanks to my neighbours, who also did whatever they could to help with feeding the little ones.

Other wild animals wandered into the yard as well.

A mama moose and her yearling; I was astonished at the size of this female moose.

On February 23, 2022. Russia launched a wide-ranging offensive against the Ukraine.

My prayers and heart went out to the innocent people and children living in the Ukraine. Since the national flower of Ukraine is the Sunflower,". I named one of the youngest fawns "Sunflower".

A Mama moose and a fawn in my front yard, looking for food and refuge.

A Mama moose eating branches and looking for food in my front yard. February 24, 2022.

Walking in the Air Lyrics

[Verse 1]
We're walking in the air
We're floating in the moonlit sky
The people far below
Are sleeping as we fly
I'm holding very tight
I'm riding in the midnight blue
I'm finding I can fly
So high above with you

[Verse 2]

Far across the world, the villages go by like
dreams
The rivers and the hills
The forests and the streams

[Bridge]
Children gaze open-mouthed
Taken by surprise
Nobody down below
Believes their eyes

[Verse 3]
We're surfing in the air
We're swimming in the frozen sky
We're drifting over icy Mountains floating by

[Bridge]
Suddenly swooping low
On an ocean deep
Rousing up a mighty monster
From his sleep

Howard Blake wrote the song "***Walking in the Air***" for the 1982 animated film "The Snowman" based on Raymond Briggs's 1978 children's book.

About the Author:

Susan Hathiramani has resided in rural Saskatchewan for the past seventeen years. She moved from the City of Saskatoon in 2004 to live in rural Saskatchewan.

Hathiramani began writing short stories when she started working at the Outlook Newspaper in 2005.

Hathiramani's second short story, **'Once Upon a Christmas',** was published in the **"Society"** volume 14. 2016, St. Peter's College, Muenster, Saskatchewan.

Hathiramani published her first fairy tale, **'The Wizard of Hawarden Book One'** in October of 2017.

On September 4, 2017, she adopted a black Lab puppy from the local animal shelter.

Leif is her companion while she is writing stories.

And she has rescued two cats. The cats are named Miska and Snipper.

Snipper loves to lay on the keyboard while Susan writes, making for some exciting typoes!

Hathiramani enjoys cooking, writing, drawing, and taking landscape photos. Her short stories and renderings are about rural Saskatchewan.

Many of her novels include Heritage homes and churches constructed in Saskatchewan around the turn of the century. Also, Susan enjoys writing short stories about anthropomorphic animals.

Susan is a Direct Care Worker at Humboldt, SK. She has worked with children in the Equine-Assisted Learning program and art programming at Nawigizigweyas Education Centre at Yellow Quill First Nation.

Also, Susan presented OSAC art programming to K-8 students at the Humboldt and District Museum and Gallery.

Susan Hathiramani

writes other stories

The Wizard of Hawarden, Book 1, *written by Susan Hathiramani, and Illustrations by Karen Zvorc Illustrations Inc. October 2017.*

The Wizard of Hawarden 2 Colouring Book*, A Saskatchewan Fairy Tale, Written by Susan Hathiramani, and Illustrations by Karen Zvorc Illustrations Inc. Published by 4 Paws Games and Publishing, Bruno Saskatchewan, Canada. 2018.*

Adaya Solves the Case of the Missing Easter Rabbit, *written by Susan Hathiramani and Illustrated by Karen Zvorc Illustrations Inc. Cover painting of the "Spring Visitor" by Sharon Eisbrenner and published by 4-Paws Games and Publishing, Bruno Saskatchewan, Canada. April 2018.*

The Wizard and Adaya Save Christmas, *written and illustrated by Susan Hathiramani. Published by Gabby Art & Books. December 2019.*

The Tale of William Rabbit, *Written and illustrated by Susan Hathiramani and published by Gabby Art & Books. April 2018.*

The Wizard's Spooky Halloween was *written and illustrated by Susan Hathiramani and published by Gabby Art & Books. 2019.*

The Wizard and the Beanstalk, *written and illustrated by Susan Hathiramani, was published by Gabby Art & Books. 2018.*

Mouseland, *by Susan Hathiramani and Karen Zvorc Illustrations Inc., published by Gabby Art & Books. 2018.*

Eaton's Once Upon a Christmas. *Written and illustrated by Susan Hathiramani. Published by Gabby Art & Books. December 2019.*

King Eilfyw. *Written by Susan Hathiramani and published by Gabby Art & Books. 2020*

Leif's First Halloween. *Written and Illustrated by Susan Hathiramani and Adaya Dosch. Published by Gabby Art & Books. 2020.*

***Grandma's Monarch Butterfly Farm.** Written and illustrated by Susan Hathiramani. Published by Gabby Art & Books. 2020.*

***A Tree Called Gabby, Book 1.** Written by Raj Hathiramani and Susan Hathiramani. Illustrations by Susan Hathiramani. Published by Gabby Art & Books. First edition, 2015.*

***A Tree Called Gabby, Book 2.** Written by Raj Hathiramani, Susan Hathiramani, and Illustrations by Karen Zvorc Illustrations Inc. In loving memory of Brody Hinz. Second edition, April 2018.*

***Gabby Book 3.** Written by Susan Hathiramani. Published by Gabby Art & Books. March 2021.*

The Wizard's Haunted Halloween at Hopkins Dining Parlour, *written by Susan Hathiramani and published by Gabby Art & Books, 2021.*

Pippin, *written and illustrated by Susan Hathiramani, published by Gabby Art & Books, 2021.*

The Wizard of Hawarden Cookbook, Book 7. By Susan Hathiramani. Published by Gabby Art & Books. 2022.